Sir Walter Raleigh

Who Was Sir Walter Raleigh - Biography, Q&A's, Timeline and Activities

Emma Thomas

Help Children Have More Fun
Discovering and Learning

It is well known that the more children interact with a topic the more they'll learn from it. Inside this book are 34 specially designed coloring images that feature key parts about the life of Sir Walter Raleigh.

Special Bonus

Buy the book today and I'll give you a link where you can print out as many copies of all the images as you want (perfect for kids and great for sharing with their friends and other students).

Plus when they want to recolor any picture, you can simply print it out and let them show off their coloring skills in new ways.

A book that never runs out...

Let their artistic expression run free and enjoy all the benefits it brings. It's widely reported that it helps improve hand to eye coordination and helps improve muscles in hands, wrists and fingers.

Plus it helps improve patience and concentration (a highly valuable skill) which can help them develop further and progress faster.

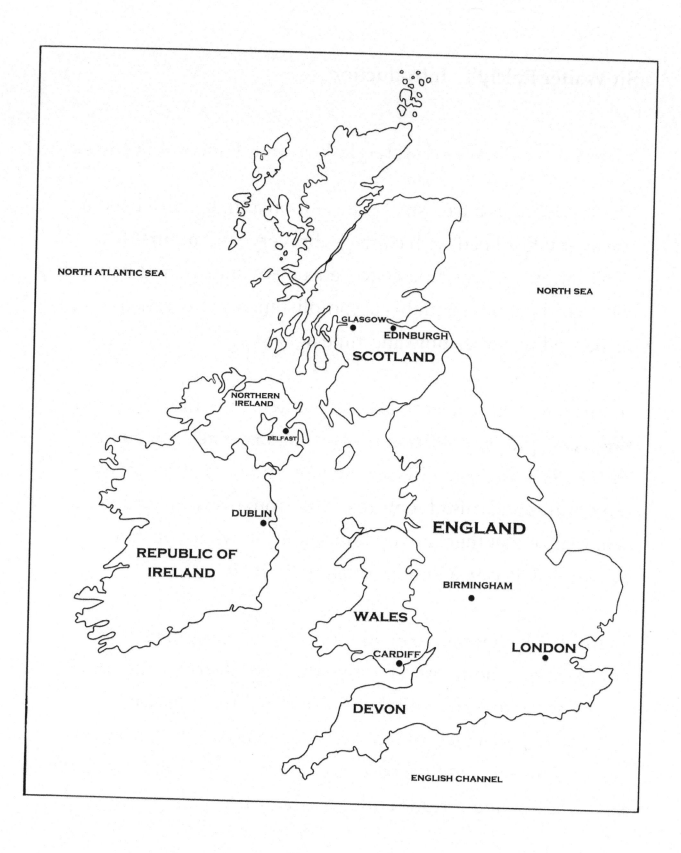

Sir Walter Raleigh - Introduction

"The Life of Sir Walter Raleigh: Explorer, Poet and Politician".

The following is a true story. Once upon a time, there lived a voyager who ebbed with courage, bravery, and a thirst for exploration. He was, in essence, a true adventurer and he marked the records of time with his accomplishments. Now, he is recounted in stories time and time again.

In this tale, you will learn about the interesting life of a famous English explorer, politician, spy, writer and poet named Sir Walter Raleigh. You will learn the ins and outs of his many adventures and misadventures. And from his wayward tales, you will realize that there are no limitations on what you can accomplish because Walter Raleigh did it all.

In this book, you will read about his early years, his family background, and how he became the adventurous individual that he is known for. You will then learn about the political relationship that he fostered with Queen Elizabeth I, how this affected his life, political power, and adventures, and how a life of such success and fortune ended so tragically.

Read along as you learn about his rise to power, his miseries and mistakes, his adventures and discoveries, his woeful and romantic poetic tunes, and his fall from grace. Such an interesting and colorful figure he truly was.

He could be graceful, charming, adventurous, smart, savvy, clever, and ambitious. But, he could also be taken over by a hunger for wealth and power, and it was this that lead to his untimely demise. In spite of this, his life is painted with brilliant stories of voyaging and travel, courage and bravery, and an innate desire to challenge the world around him.

Chapter 1: His Early Years

Walter Raleigh was born in Devon, England to his mother and father, who were named Walter Raleigh and Catherine Champernowne. The specific details of his earliest years remain somewhat unclear to historians and many lingering questions remain.

However, at some point in his early life, he chose to travel to Ireland and participate in the rebellions that were transpiring at the time. Even during his earliest years, he proved to be a valiant young spirit who challenged those all around him. It was this very tenacious spirit of his that enabled him to accomplish everything that he achieved during his life.

Whether he was in England, or in Ireland, he made change everywhere he landed. In fact, he went so far as to own a property in Ireland itself. As powerful as he was in his early life, he established small plots of power during his earliest years, as a precursor to what he would do in the future.

What did this small plot of land symbolize in his eyes? Aside from power, it symbolized ownership, ownership over his own environment, one that he could transform to his own liking, a place in which he could conduct himself according to his own rules and authority.

Later in his life, he would be a politician, so this was a great start for him. Another reason why this choice to own land in Ireland was so interesting is because he was born into a protestant family.

At the time, the country of Ireland was a Catholic country, and Protestants, although Christian, do not agree with Catholics in many ways. This showed his desire to go beyond his comfort zone, what he was used to, and this is the hallmark of a true explorer. It seems that Sir Walter Raleigh began his adventures early on, in small ways, and he had the innate need to venture out into uncomfortable territory.

But even before these small conquests, he was a boy, a small boy baffled and intrigued by the vast world around him. He was raised in a small farmhouse in a village in Devon England, and he was the youngest in his family.

His humble beginnings would differ starkly from the fortune that he would encounter in the future. However, even though he was raised on a farm, this did not deter him from having big visions about what he wanted to accomplish in the future.

With 4 brothers and sisters, there was always much to do, he delved into much exploration in his childhood innocence. The brothers and sister were the product of two different marriages, and his half brothers would also find their way into the records of history by gaining political power in their adulthood. His half-brothers and brother were Humphrey Gilbert, John Gilbert, Carew Raleigh and Adrian Gilbert.

Being a Protestant family at this time was not easy, especially considering the ongoing conflicts between the Catholics and the Protestants. In fact, the issue was so profound that his family had to hide during the reign of a Catholic Queen, named Queen Mary I. They were very loyal to their Protestant views, and Walter Raleigh's father actually took shelter in a tower in order to avoid being executed for his Protestant beliefs. It was during this time that Raleigh began to strongly dislike Catholics and the religion itself. He expressed his hatred for that religion once Queen Elizabeth I took the throne in 1558.

As Raleigh grew older, he became more courageous, as well. In fact, he began military service, which would be a harbinger for future victories in his interesting life. He developed the will and the capacity to fight valiantly, like a warrior at this time. In 1569, he travelled to France, in order to participate in the Civil wars in France, providing his military service. He specifically served with the Huguenots.

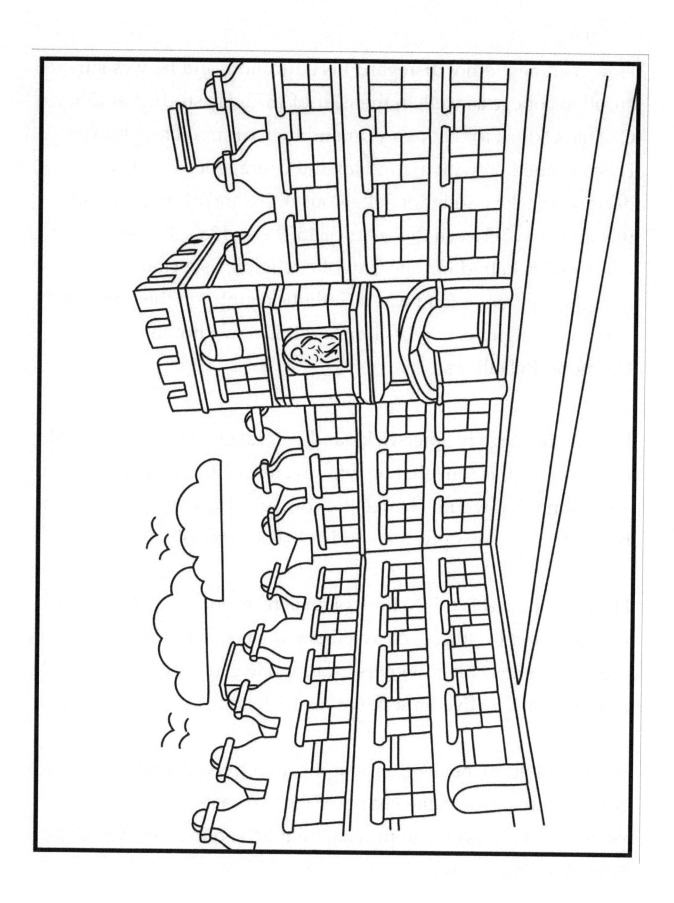

However, he did not disregard his education, and he was sure to enroll in college as well, in the year of 1572. He studied at Oriel College Oxford for about a year and then dropped out, however. He continued on with his valiant and courageous spirit, and decided to take part in the rebellions of Ireland at the time, and this occurred between the years of 1579 and 1583. This was a far cry from his hatred for The Catholic religion, especially considering that Ireland was a Catholic country at the time. This was a very significant rebellion, and it is now known as the Desmond Rebellions.

During the Siege of Smerwick, land was taken over and divided up. It was at this time that he was given something amazing, something that would change the course of the entire life that lay before him. He was given an entire 40,000 acres of land.

How much land is this? Think of an acre as one big field. Now, multiply that by 40,000. At least in an area called Munster, he was one of the biggest landowners around. He even convinced people from England to live on some of his Irish land, as well.

For 17 full years, he lived as a landlord in Ireland, and even became the mayor in the year of 1588. He was so wealthy at one point, that he was able to purchase a mansion in town, which he named Myrtle Grove.

Myrtle Grove was a beautiful, rustic mansion that was characteristic of the time, and it had many Medieval qualities to it. It was almost castle like in appearance, but was small and modest enough for someone to call home.

During this time, Raleigh made a friend named Edmund Spenser, who was from England, and they travelled quite a bit together.

They frequently travelled all the way from Ireland to England, and it was during this time that Raleigh delved deeper into his literary and poetry interests.

Unfortunately, however, Raleigh's fortune was short lived and there were some issues with the land he owned in Ireland. But during their travels, Spenser introduced one of his poems, Faerie Queene in the presence of Elizabeth I. Eventually, by the year of 1602, he decided to sell the estates to Richard Boyle.

It was during his early years that he had a preview of his future, in which he would find fortune and pursue wealth in other ways. While his initial destiny was not to become a landlord for the rest of his life, he would find most of his success in the political world, and in expeditions, as well. He lived the life of a fearless adventurer, and during this time, his journey had only just begun. After he gained favor from the Queen, opportunities continued to open and he would relish those opportunities to pursue those dreams.

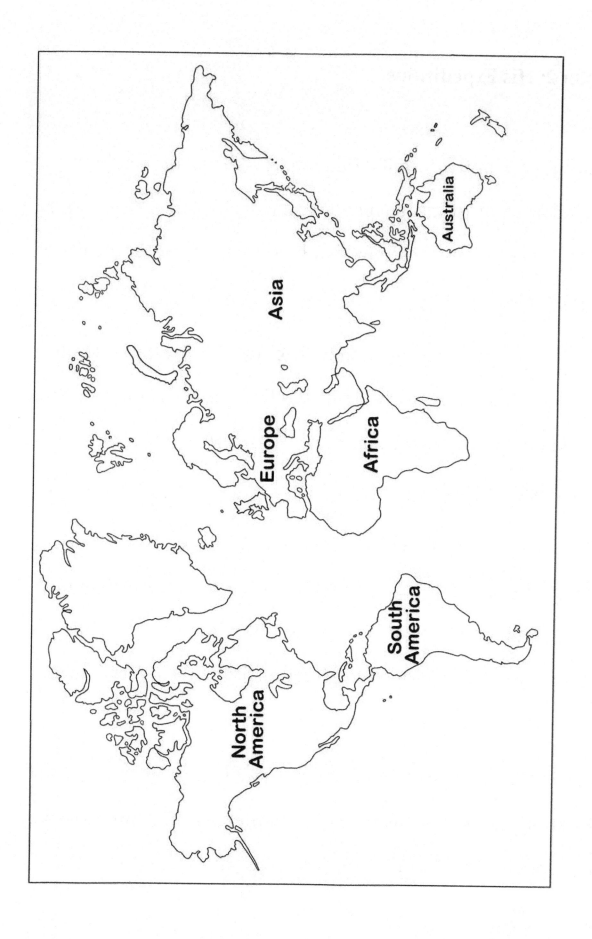

Chapter 2: His Expeditions

If anything can aptly describe Raleigh, it is the term "Explorer". He loved adventure, just as he did as a child. He like adventures for many reasons, and it seems that he was destined for the life of an explorer from birth.

To make his expeditions even more exciting, Sir Walter Raleigh did not just limit his fun adventures to Europe. He actually travelled all the way to the American continent, even before the United States existed.

What does it take for one to become an adventurer of sorts? Well, at least in his case, it takes quite a bit of determination, resistance and even ambition to be an adventurer. Not to mention, while everyone experiences some fear, fear cannot be the overarching emotion for an explorer like himself.

He never allowed fear to impede his desire for travel and exploration and it was this very quality that allowed him to delve ever deeper into the North American continent.

In the 1580s, Raleigh was interested in something called the New World. Where did the idea of the New World come from? From a man named Amerigo Vespucci, who decided that the lands that Christopher Columbus found in 1492 were not Asia, but rather a "New World".

The discovery of this "New World" led to the attainment of gold and silver, new materials, new crops, and new forms of medicine, as well. Raleigh did not shy away from the New World and he was brave enough to explore regions such as North Carolina and Florida. This was his very first expedition to America, and during this time, he coined the term "Virgina" to pay homage to the Virgin Queen.

After this first adventure of his, he did not stop there. He decided to go on another exploration of the New World, and when he did this, his first stop was Roanoke Island. He made his very own settlement there, and he brought people with him. He stayed there for some time, and he sailed back to England because he needed more items to give his new colony a healthy start.

He promised that after a year, he would come back with more supplies from England. But, he did not live up to this promise, and it took three years to return. This was a critical mistake on his part, one that would be echoed throughout history. While it was a brave attempt to begin a new settlement, more planning should have been taken into consideration.

There was a reason why his return took so long. At the time, The Spanish Armada posed a threat to Great Britain and Queen Elizabeth I wanted to use all ships to defend them against the Spanish Armada. After they finally defeated them, Raleigh was allowed to sail back to the U.S. However, the journey back was not as easy as they were hoping for it to be. This is because they decided to go to Cuba in order to find more riches in that area.

However, eventually they came back to Roanoke, but there was just one problem-there were no more settlers there waiting for them. The colonists had disappeared, and they have no idea where they were. What a mystery this was too poor Raleigh, for he wished to expand his colony, and regretted the three year wait

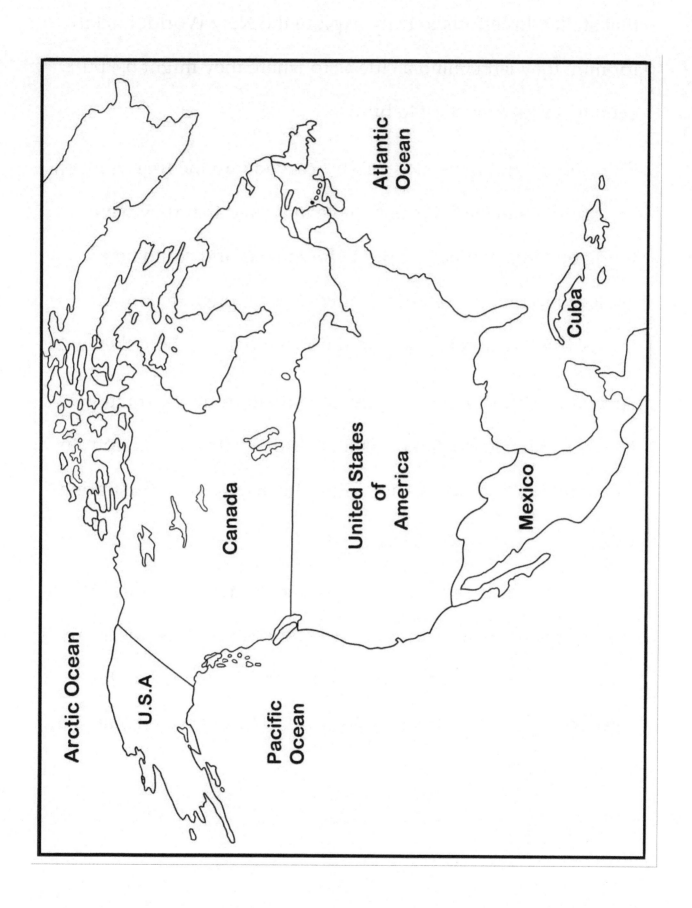

that stalled his efforts to truly explore the New World. Luckily, for him, they left behind a clue as to where they might be, but even this was a mystery to him.

They left behind the words "CRO" carved into the tree trunk on their settlement, and this may have indicated that they were living on Croatoan Island. But before this island could be explored to find the settlers, a hurricane erupted, making it impossible to sail safely to find the survivors. So, there they were.

After the Spanish Armada prevented them from returning in a timely fashion to Roanoke Island, and they went on a detour to Cuba in search of riches, they found themselves in a frustrating position.

Had the colonists settled elsewhere and started a new life? Were they swept out by sea? Were they captured? They pondered these notions for a bit. No one truly knows what happened at this settlement, and it is now referred to as "The Lost Colony at Roanoke Island."

Raleigh had the intention to colonize in 1584, but he didn't reach his goal after this mishap at Roanoke Island. Although this was a failure, he was a great inspiration to future aspiring colonists who wanted to explore the depths of the New World. Furthermore, he engaged in future expeditions of the area, and he and his companions were able to pay for these explorations. Unfortunately, he did not have enough money to start a successful colony in North America.

Where did his fortune go, and why didn't the Queen patronize more colonies with a good number of resources? Not all of these questions can be answered in their entirety, but chances are, she had to spend most of the resources on defending England against the Spanish. Furthermore, much of Raleigh's own fortune began to dwindle because he managed it poorly when he had opportunities for growth. Many of his expeditions were self funded, but with enough resources it is thought he could have started a successful colony.

Chapter 3: Later Years

During his later years, Raleigh decided to return to England in 1581, and he took a very special interest in the court life at the time. The reason why he expressed an interest in the Court Life is because he was especially interested in the Protestant Church.

Along with this, he began to gain the approval and the acceptance of Queen Elizabeth I, and he was eventually knighted, which was a considerable honor at the time. He was also given the title of warden, and vice admiral, as well. Clearly, his career in politics was flourishing.

During this time in his life, his political power gradually began to increase. It was around this time that the previously mentioned expeditions and exploits began.

It seems that for Sir Walter Raleigh, the 1580s were a time of great influence, power and exploration. Although his attempt to venture into North America proved to be a failure, in terms of setting up a colony, he left a large imprint and paved the way for

future explorers. And just as he ventured successfully to North America, he played a large role in the political atmosphere of England at the time.

`He was a member of the parliament from 1585 to 1586, and it was at this time that he was allowed to colonize America. It seems that his growing political power at the time gave him the ability to explore the New World and expand his influence on the globe.

His political power also gave him the wherewithal and the resources to go on this exploration across the sea. During this time, a shipbuilder named R. Chapman built a ship so that he could sail the Atlantic to the new world.

Queen Elizabeth absolutely adored him, and she bestowed him with the honor of many cherished rewards. One of the rewards was the Durham House, which was located in Dorset.

Another reward was becoming Captain of the Yeoman of the Guard. His political relationship with Queen Elizabeth I opened him up to a world of different opportunities, and helped him expand his power also. After he became the Vice Admiral in 1588, he oversaw the defense of the coast.

During his later years, he would also wed a woman, someone who was well acquainted with the Queen. Her name was Elizabeth Throckmorton, and she was pregnant, as well.

Raleigh was 11 years older than her, and her nickname was Bess. She had a son who later passed away because of the plague in 1592. Bess's main job was to be the lady in waiting for the Queen and to serve her, as always. However, the Queen did not approve this marriage, and when she discovered it, she sent Raleigh and Bess to prison in 1592.

That year, however, they were both released so that he could pursue his explorations once again and set up an expedition. The Queen needed his help because at the time, the Spanish were growing in power and they wanted to attack the coast of Spain. But even after this, his political relationship with the Queen remained strained, but he committed himself to Bess. Even when Raleigh had to depart on one of his travels or expedition, Bess was very effective at managing the household. They also had sons named Water and Carew.

At the time, Raleigh probably assumed that his legal troubles would deem in ineligible for future participation in politics, and that his adventures would be over. But, in spite of going to prison in 1592, something amazing happened. In 1593, he became a member of parliament, and he retired the following year.

During this time, he built a new house, and he made many friends as well. One day, however, during a dinner party, he debated about religion, and some began to spread rumors that he was an atheist, which was not true in any way. He was eventually charged with atheism, but still managed to get elected to Parliament. During this time in politics, he was very vocal about his views on religion.

This showed special courage, especially since there was so much religious conflict at the time. Remember, as a child, his father faced execution because of his religious stance. But even as an adult, he did not allow the mishaps of the past to get in the way

of his voice and opinion, and it is because of this that he was elected to parliament.

In the year of 1595, he explored South America in search of a legendary city known as El Dorado. When he finally returned to England in 1596, he wrote of his adventures in Venezuela, in which he attempted to find this legendary city in a book called *The Discovery of Guiana.*

However, there is one element of this book that appears to be fictitious. It was historical, by all accounts, but several things were embellished, or exaggerated, in terms of what he had discovered there. It appears that Sir Raleigh had a penchant for both discovery and for imagination, as well.

While he claims that he was able to find gold, no one was able to confirm this. He also wrote that he found Angel Falls, but this was later discovered to be false, as well. In 1596, however, he undertook another vast leap, one that was military in nature. He participated in what is now known as the Capture of Cadiz, in 1596. However, his courage came at cost, and he was actually injured at this time. He knew that this was a possibility, however,

but his bravery did not stop him from future ventures. For example, the following year, was appointed the second in command during the Island Voyages, on his way to the Azores. Truly, he understood the meaning of leadership and did not allow the prospect of injury or defeat to deter him from his missions.

In 1597, he once again became a member of parliament. However, this time, it was for Dorset. A few years later, in 1601, he entered the Parliament in Cornwall. He did something that was rarely, if ever done, at the time. He sat on Parliament in three separate counties, and he had clearly spread his political influence. From the years of 1600 6o 1603, he served as a Governor of Jersey and he was able to strengthen its security and defenses, as well. For example, he had a fort constructed in the region.

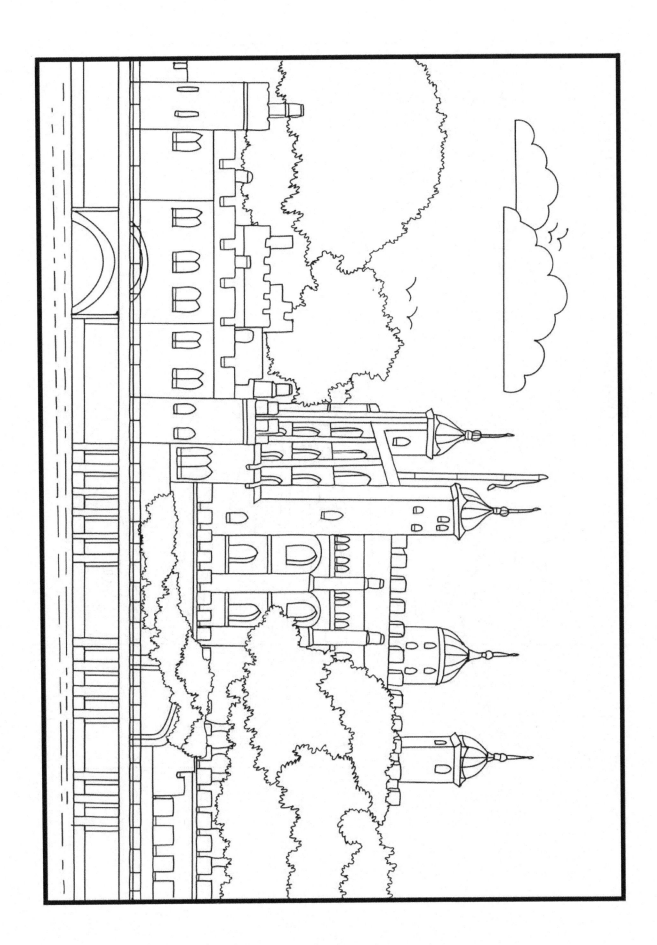

Chapter 4: Legal Troubles

At the time, Raleigh had established a much better political relationship with Queen Elizabeth, and he received her Royal favor. She played a critical role throughout the years in all of his conquests, explorations and political roles that he served.

However, in 1603, she passed away, and everything began to change. He no longer had the shroud of security that he had before this. He was arrested shortly after her death in 1603, and he was imprisoned in the Tower of London. They tried him for treason, because he participated in a set up against King James.

In spite of their claims, Raleigh continued to defend himself, however, the prosecution presented a confession that was obviously his, one that divulged all of the details he had plotted against King James.

According to Raleigh, there was no official evidence against him, and that there were no solid facts in the case, at all. Of course, documents that were later found seemed to prove the theory that

Raleigh participated in a plot against King James. Not only did he dislike King James, but he actually wanted the Spanish Invasion to happen. It was at this time that he became a spy for the Spanish, which was an unwise move on his part.

In exchange for becoming a Spanish spy, he received a sum of money from them. However, after years of serving England on parliament, and having his expeditions funded by an English Queen, he ultimately betrayed his nation. It is because of this that he was imprisoned.

Many people glorify the career of a spy, especially in movies. But in real life, spying can hurt one's country and compromise its safety.

Until the year of 1616, he remained imprisoned. However, he did not allow his years in prison to go to waste and he wrote quite a bit?

During this time not only did he wrote several treatises, but he also wrote the first portion of The History of the World, which was eventually published in 1628. This book, which had its first volume written in prison, was about the ancient world, specifically Ancient Greece and Rome. In 1604, when he was still imprisoned, his son Carew was born.

THE HISTORY   OF THE WORLD

In 1616, Raleigh was finally release after a long stint in prison. However, this was done under one condition. He had to explore Venezuela once again in order to locate the legendary city, El Dorado.

However, during this time, his adventures would involve far more than mere exploration, and they would instead entail an attack of a Spanish outpost. He was able to accomplish this because he and his fellow voyagers were under the authority of Lawrence Keymis.

All of this happened on the Orinoco River, and it was not easy to find El Dorado without conflict from Spanish explorers.

During the first attack, Raleigh lost someone of immense value to him, his son Walter. His son was shot and eventually passed away from the wounds. Not only was this a blow to Raleigh's goals, but it was an irreversible loss that plunged him into deep sorrow.

Upon Raleigh's return to England, his luck became progressively worse. After suffering the untimely death of his son, he too would be taken before his time.

Count Gondomar, who was a Spanish Ambassador, was infuriated about Raleigh's expedition, and insisted that he have his death sentence restored. He was able to persuade King James to have Raleigh executed. While he made several attempts to escape his potential execution, he failed in every attempt. It appears that this was the end of the road for him. After leaving behind a legacy of literature, innovation, exploration, adventure, and politics, he was to face a grim execution.

On October 29, 1618, Raleigh was beheaded at the Palace of Westminster. But, even before his execution, he did not cower in fear. He informed the executioner that he wanted to be remembered for his bravery, not as a coward. Even as the executioner hesitated, he urged him to carry out the beheading. Even shortly before his death, he showed a high degree of fearlessness and courage, and her life reflected partly on this.

After he was executed, the searched his cell, and they found a patch of tobacco, and on the patch, he wrote the tobacco was his best friend during his miserable imprisonment. To make matters worse, his wife received his embalmed head in the mail, while his body was buried. This was certainly a morbid way to remember one's husband but this was characteristic at the time. His final resting place was Beddington, Surrey. 29 years after Raleigh died, his wife then passed away. Afterwards his head was transferred to his grave.

At one time in his life, he received the favor of Queen Elizabeth I. However, after she died, he lost his popularity and was no longer the celebrated figure that he once was. Of course, in spite of the fact that many people disliked him, they disagreed with his execution. To many, it seemed unfair. Even a judge at his trial noted that the English legal system was very corrupt and that the action taken against Sir Walter Raleigh was unfair. However, documents later recovered suggest that there was a strong case against him.

Chapter 6: His Legacy

Sir Walter Raleigh lived on in his legacy, even after his death. This is the hallmark of a true leader, a true explorer who persists throughout history. Many people defied, rebelled and explored during his time.

However, only a few obtained enough recognition necessary to live on throughout time, have monuments erected in their name, cities named after them, and their works discussed in books in the modern world. Not only did he make quite the impression on the people of his time, but individuals are still talking about him today.

The capital of North Carolina is Raleigh, and it is named after him because he explored and established Roanoke Colony. This was one of the honors given to him in an effort to uphold the legacy that he left on the Earth. While some of explorations did not go as smoothly as planned, with some just being utter failures, there were successes. There was even a bronze statue placed there in his honor, and homage is paid to the Lost Colony, as well.

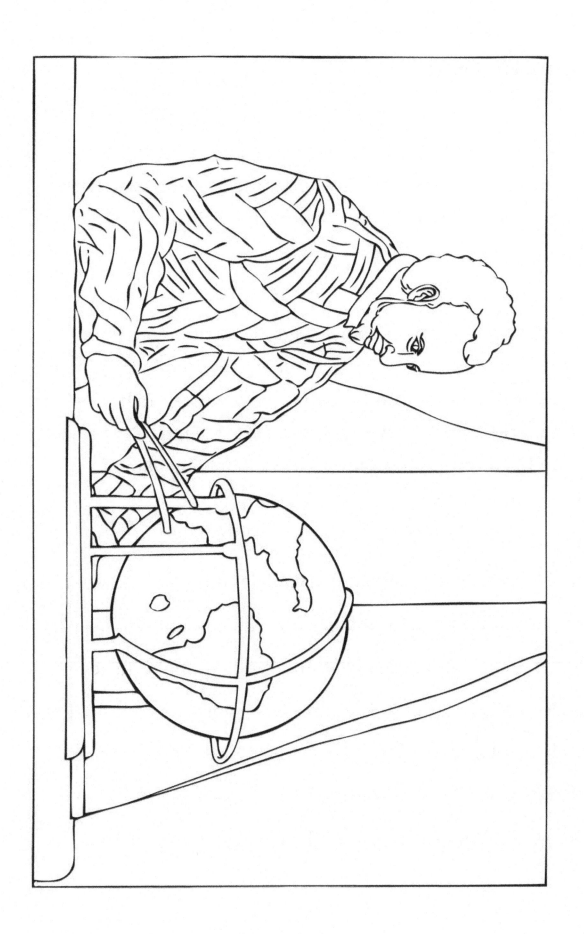

Therefore, none have forgotten the sacrifices he made, the valiance he showed, and his adventurous spirit throughout his life. He had an influence that was not restricted by time, or by continents.

The fact that monuments now exist in the United States honoring him shows that he was more than just an Englishman who was a part of Parliament in the 1500s and 1600s. He was someone who truly did change the world.

Many other places have been named in his honor, including Raleigh County, a boarding house in North Carolina, and Mount Raleigh, which is located in Canada. Additionally, there is a Raleigh Glacier and Raleigh Creek. There is also a Mount Gilbert that is named after his step brother, Sir Humphrey. Cities and mountains are named after him, and this can be viewed from a symbolic standpoint. Mountains are majestic and cities are grand. Obviously, he was a majestic and grand as the mountains and city named after him.

Many people tend to believe that the potato was transported to Europe from North America by Sir Raleigh. Clearly, the potato had a dramatic impact on the continent of Europe, and some countries lived on this as their primary food source.

However, some disagree firmly with this, and do not think it would have been feasible for him to discover the potato at all, especially since he explored only a few regions of North America.

What would Sir Walter Raleigh think if he were to learn of his legacy? Would he be satisfied with what he achieved during his life? Would he have regrets? Or would he be at peace with the life that he lived and the depth to which he explored North America? The answers to these questions may never be known, but the influence he had on exploration will always be mentioned in history.

Chapter 7: Written Works

Raleigh wrote books, documents, as well as poems. What is interesting about his poems is that they do not contain flowery language, nor are they difficult to understand. They are actually composed in very simplistic language, and they are incredibly straight forward.

One of the reasons why this is so important is because at the time, there were certain influences that had an impact on poets everywhere, such as the Italian Renaissance. In spite of this, he did not allow the Renaissance to influence his writing and he made sure that it remained simple and straightforward.

Most of his writing is situated around a few important themes, including beauty, time, love, etc. He drew a lot of his thematic inspiration from the Medieval times, thereby expressing dislike for the world. Most poets during the Renaissance did not do this.

During his imprisonment, he happened to write poems there as well. He even engaged in poetic responses to other poets.

All of his poetry was very simple, and some may criticize him for this. However, it should be noted that poetry does not have to be extremely complicated in order to be considered important, or to be considered a work of art. Just as he was able to redefine what it meant to be an explorer at the time, he was able to redefine the art of poetry by showing that he did not have to adhere to poetic trends at the time.

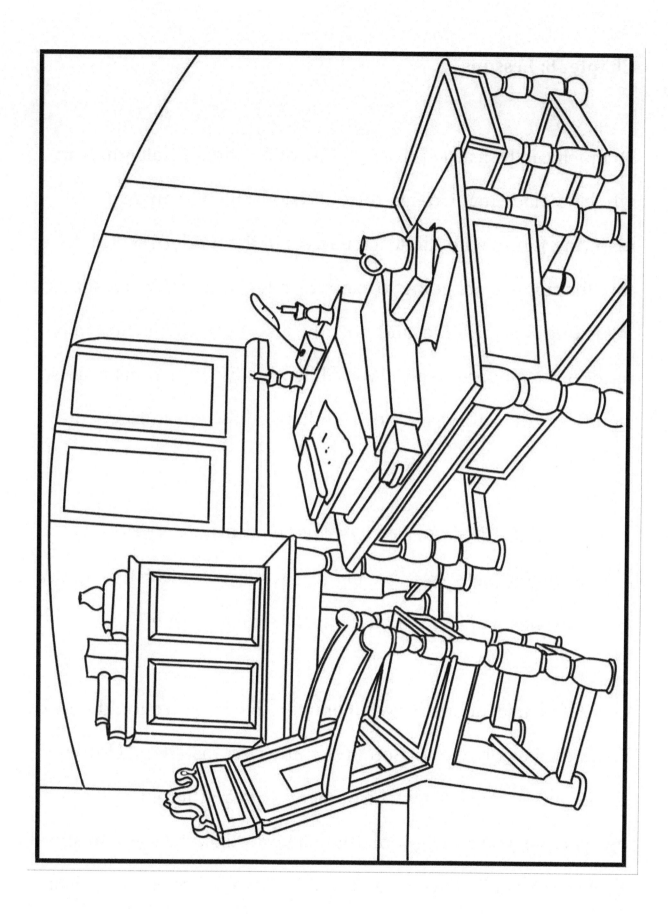

Chapter 8: Lessons

So much can be learned from the life of Sir Walter Raleigh. And while he made many dangerous decisions, he was an awe inspiring figure who can teach us a lot in the modern world. In this chapter, we are going to examine a few important questions, regarding Raleigh's life, and how the lessons from his life can be used in the modern world. We will learn why his actions were so significant in history, and how he changed the world forever.

1. *As discussed, Sir Raleigh wrote certain materials in prison, including books, treatises, and poems. What lessons can be learned from this, and how can this be applied to a modern life?*

Of course, no matter what era you live in, you should never break the law or go to prison under any circumstances. However, if you look at Raleigh's imprisonment from a different perspective, you realize something a key lesson that we can all apply to our daily lives. Even though he was trapped in a prison for several years, he continued to express himself and have a voice. He wrote books and poems, and he was productive during this time, even though the prison walls restricted where he was able to go. There will be occasions in life when your situation or circumstances will not be ideal. You may not be able to travel where you want to travel, or do what you want to do. You may not live in the best of environments and you may be upset by the things around you.

However, what you can learn from Walter Raleigh is that in spite of this, you can still do your best. He was able to compose countless poems, and even books that he would later publish. The wonderful lesson that we can learn from him is that there is never any excuse to not be inventive or innovative in any way. The circumstances around you cannot dictate where you will go in life, or what you can accomplish. You can be productive and creative, even when you do not like the environment around you.

Everyone has situations that they wish they could change, but some situations cannot be changed right away. So, no matter where you are in life, do you best, and you will get to the next best moment.

During his nights in prison, Sir Walter Raleigh was most likely very discouraged and saddened at times. However, he kept his spirits up just enough so that he could use his voice for good, even within the confines of a prison. It takes quite a bit of character, to do your very best, and express yourself creatively, even when your circumstances are not ideal. In Raleigh's case, he had to be mentally strong, persistent, and ambitious. It is probably already clear that he harnessed these character traits throughout his life in order to accomplish what he did. With these character traits, you can accomplish quite a bit because virtually every challenge in life requires that you possess strength, persistence and ambition. So, if you can master this, no situation can be too difficult to overcome for you in the future.

Raleigh defied the Queen's orders and married a pregnant woman. What lessons can one learn from this?

During this time, marriage was something that had to be authorized by the Queen. Even today, we live in a society where others try to put restraints on love and who can marry whom. In Raleigh's case, his society was much stricter back then. However, from this, a critical lesson can be learned, that you should follow your heart if you genuinely love something. Whether this is a musical instrument, sport, or even a subject matter that you like, you should follow your dreams- even if it seems unusual to others.

For example, everyone in your class may play piano. However, you may have a special interest in the Tuba. If this is something that really captivates you, you should not worry how others will perceive you. Instead, you should pursue what you love if it is truly one of your passions. In Raleigh's case he loved his wife so much that he did not fear imprisonment. Of course, you should never pursue a passion that is illegal, of course.

What character traits did Sir Walter Raleigh possess, and how did this help him pursue what he truly loved, in spite of the odds and the judgment that he would receive? He persevered, and he kept his mind focused on his love and his passion. This is an important trait to harness, especially if you want to filter out distractions and succeed at what you truly love to do. During his life, Raleigh expressed these qualities in romance, as well as his expeditions. He always challenged certain norms around him.

2. *In what ways did Raleigh's upbringing transform him into the daring explorer that he was?*

Raleigh's upbringing played a significant role in shaping the individual that he became. During his adulthood, he showed defiance, as well as adventure, persistence, bravery, independent thinking, creativity, and bravery, as well. His earliest years helped transform him into the person he became for a number of different reasons.

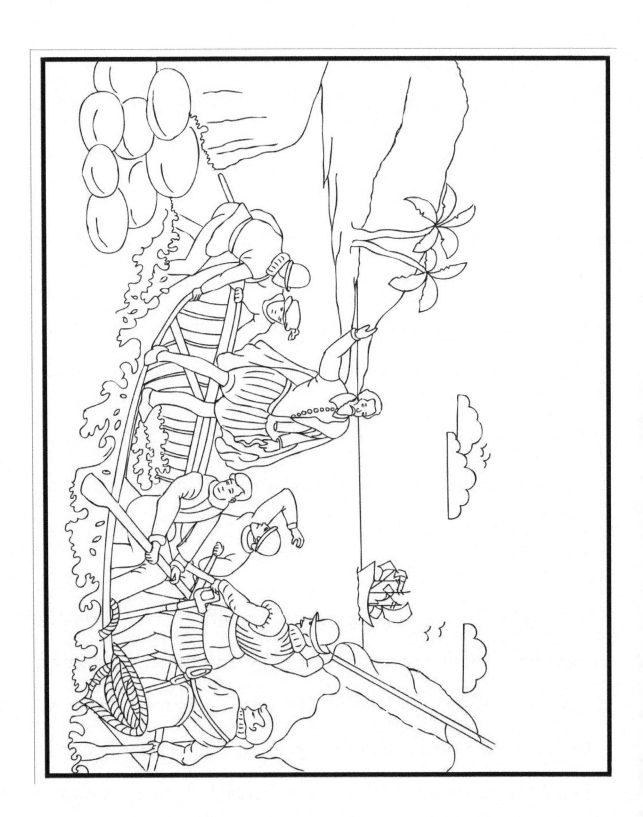

Even as a child, he understood what it meant to defy the norm. In his childhood, his family was adamantly opposed to Catholicism, and this shaped some of his future religious views.

Their opposition almost got them in trouble, and his father was even forced to hide in a Tower, as he feared that he would be executed. With this said, he learned about defiance and rebellion at an early age. During his early years, he even participated in the military, as well. Based on this information, it is easy to understand how he developed an interest in exploring the world, and doing the unthinkable.

Through his life, he defied the norm on many occasions, leaving some people very angry and disgruntled by his behavior. When he attacked a Spanish Fort during his later years on a visit to Venezuela, he infuriated many different people, and this partly accounts for his execution. After Queen Elizabeth I died, he participated in a plot against King James, and this caused him to lose popularity and favor, and it sent him back to prison for some time. Furthermore, when he participated as a spy, this also set him back in his attempts to keep his status and prominence.

Of course, it is always recommended that one respect their authority figures, and this is a skill that one should retain well into adulthood. However, there is an undeniable significance here in what Sir Walter Raleigh did. While you should respect authority figures, such as teachers and parents, sometimes, one must go against the grain, or what is considered normal, in order to make changes. This is completely fine, as long as it is respectful, legal and does not disrupt the peace.

There are peaceful ways in which you can be an independent thinker and question something that you do not think is right. As you can see, this aided Sir Walter Raleigh greatly in his adulthood, especially since it helped him become a successful writer and poet, explorer, spy, and much more.

If you use this particular quality in the right way, it can work to your advantage. It is important to go against the grain in a respectful and peaceful way, and this can be observed throughout history. Some individuals, of course, did not go about this so peacefully. However, it was their different train of thought that led the world to another dimension of knowledge.

People in history have had to challenge the norm in order to make advancements in science, exploration, etc. If no one ever challenged authority in some sense, there would never be any change. Therefore, do not be afraid to think outside the box, as long as it is law abiding and respectful.

3. *What did Raleigh's final display of bravery (shortly before his execution) symbolize*

Shortly before Sir Walter Raleigh was executed, he made a very important statement. He let the executioner know that before he died, he wanted to let the world know that he displayed bravery, even in the midst of an execution. Furthermore, he urged the executioner to proceed with the beheading.

Raleigh was certainly overwhelmed with fear at the time. No one would be completely calm and courageous if they were facing such a fate. However, he maintained his composure, and he made sure that his final words were those of a brave individual. He understood that his fate was sealed, and that there was nothing he could do to change the present circumstances.

What lessons can we glean from this, and how can this be applied to the context of everyday life? Essentially, there are events in our lives that are the way that they are, and they cannot be immediately changed. Raleigh recognized that in that moment, his fate was sealed.

Similarly, we will have to confront situations in life that cannot be presently changed, situations that must be accepted as they are. For example, if you receive a poor grade on an assignment, and you fear how this will affect you progress, you may come to the conclusion that there is nothing you can do about that specific grade.

However, referring back to the words of Walter Raleigh, how can one handle this situation? You should not cringe in fear, or be afraid for your future. Instead, you should be brave and courageous enough to seek out the help you need, study harder, and try harder next time.

Even before his execution, he did not cease to show bravery and acceptance of his circumstances. Sometimes, you must accept where you are and exhibit bravery in order to proceed to the next best point.

It almost seems as though Raleigh was a fearless individual, given the way that he handled himself. However like all others, he was a human being who was faced with the same difficulties and miseries as your everyday individual. He had fear, sorrow, and all other emotions that humans typically experienced.

However, what truly distinguishes him from the rest was the manner in which channeled his fears and frustrations. For example, he confronted the issues with bravery. Instead of wallowing in self pity while in prison, he wrote works that would eventually be published. Instead of backing down from unexplored territory, out of fear of the unknown, he ventured further into unknown lands. And instead of blindly following certain religious values, he voiced his opinion.

4 - *He chose not to draw inspiration from everyday Renaissance poets. Instead, he rebelled against this and wrote in a simplistic style. What lessons can be gleaned from this?*

This is just one of many ways that he held onto his roots, and defied the expectations and opinions of those around him. As you have probably already realized, Raleigh had a habit of thinking independently and creatively, and going against the grain.

When he explored the depths of Venezuela, he ventured against the grain of what was common at this time. When he vowed to create a colony of his own, he had lofty dreams that were a far cry from the typical person of his day.

He went from the humble beginnings of a young Protestant child, to someone who won the favor of the Queen. Furthermore, in spite of the rising Catholic influence of his time, he remained firmly rooted in his Protestant views and did not allow anyone to sway him

otherwise. He was not the easiest person in the world to influence. And, when he had a goal or an ambition, he went along with it, in spite of any disapproval that he received.

His ambitious, and often, defiant spirit made its way into his written works, especially in his poetry. Many people of the time were influenced by the Renaissance in their art and poetry, and during this time, they believed in speaking highly of mankind.

However, he chose not to be influenced by this and instead decided that he must stick to his pastoral roots, and much of his work reminds readers of the Medieval times. It talks about chivalry, love, and time. It is very simple, speaking highly of love, and ill of the world around him.

Sometimes, it is important to venture out of what is considered normal and conventional, from an artistic perspective. In the art world, many of the most respected people create change in their field by thinking differently, or by doing something that was not widely accepted. It is with this very defiance that people have been able to shed light on a new perspective in the art world. Even today, Sir Walter Raleigh's work is respected, and other literary geniuses commended him on his work.

The fact that he did not go along with a Renaissance inspiration enabled him to stand out from other poets of the time. He stood out because many of the Renaissance poets spent their time glorifying humanity and speaking highly of human beings and their accomplishments. Whereas, his poetry showed a more simplistic portrayal of life.

He looked to very simple things with inspiration, including land, time, love, and simple romance. He made sure that his work was not diluted by overly complicated language, or by unnecessary themes. He stuck to universal themes that everyone could relate to.

By adulthood, most people can relate to things such as time and love, regardless of what their political stance, religion, or nationality. His adventurous spirit truly echoed throughout these works because he did not feel the need to be conventional and to do what all the other writers were doing. The hallmark of a true poet and artist is someone who can change the trends of their time.

4. Here is a verse from one of Raleigh's poems:

But could youth last, and love still breed, Had joys no date, nor age no need, Then these delights my mind might move, To live with thee and be thy Love."

What does this reveal about his life, or who he was as a person? In one of his poems, Raleigh expressed some common themes about love and time, and each verse appears to be very significant.

Many of his poems were written in prison, and he probably found a great solace in these literary works. In this particular poem verse, although there are only four lines, there is so much material that one can analyze. In the first line, he goes back to the theme that has been discussed previously, time. This is something that was very common in medieval poetry.

He poses a question about youth and age, and he discusses love, as well. But for the most part, he appears to be very fixated on love in this poem. This shows a strikingly different side of him than one that was often portrayed in historical accounts.

In historical accounts, we see him as the defiant explorer, the spy, and a man who held political power. In these accounts, very rarely do we see his poetic side, the side of him that spoke of love and romance. Clearly, he was a far more complex character than initially thought.

7. *What do you think his betrayals of England and Spain suggest?*

During his lifetime, he appears to have experienced conflict with both the Spanish, and with the English as well. So, what does this reveal about him?

This reveals that he did not feel particularly bound by nationality. In fact, many of his own personal pursuits seemed to trump the desires of his nation. However, he did do quite a bit to help England, in terms of donating his fleet to defeat the Spanish army, and so on.

8. *How do you think he felt when his colony at Roanoke failed?*

How he felt about the failure at Roanoke can only be put into words he probably by Raleigh himself. But like anyone, he had a typical response to the failure. He probably felt saddened, frustrated, and very dismayed by the apparent failure.

Furthermore, he probably reflected on where he went wrong and how he could have come about it differently. However, he had a warrior's spirit, and this mistake did not stop him from pursuing future ventures.

Clearly, this did not discourage him from future explorations of the world because even after this failure at Roanoke, he ventured into Cuba, South America, and vowed to find legendary cities. Clearly, this was just the inception of his expeditions and he clearly had a thirst for more adventure.

9. Do you think he deserves the monuments and honors that he received after his death?

It would be reasonable to say that he was not by any means a perfect person. He had his faults, he served time in prison, he was accused of treason, and ultimately he was executed. He spied on his own nation, and he even attacked a Spanish Fort after being a spy for the Spanish. Clearly, he was not someone who respected authority at all times. However, in spite of this mistake, he did some groundbreaking things that helped change the course of history. He most certainly deserves the monuments and honors that were created in his name. Firstly, he became a major landlord in Ireland, one of the most prominent at the time.

Furthermore, he was able to win the favor of Queen Elizabeth, in spite of his religious upbringing. He married a woman who was already pregnant, instead of judging her and deeming her unworthy. These acts alone show that he was far different from the rest.

Along with everything mentioned above, he served on apolitical chair in three different counties, and he wrote commendable works while he served time in prison. However, of all of his accomplishments, his expeditions appear to receive the most praise, out of all of them. For example, in addition to selling to Roanoke, he ventured off into Cuba with his fleet to find riches.

Along with this, he travelled deep into South America to find legendary cities, and to find riches there as well. Somehow, he was able to establish very powerful partnerships with both England and with Spain, even though he betrayed them both in the end. Hence, while he made his share of mistakes, he paved the pathway for future explorers, wrote prolifically, and never lost his courage. For this reason, he does deserve the honors that were made in his name.

10. What were some of his biggest mistakes?

Like all human beings, Sir Walter Raleigh made his decent share of mistakes during his lifetime. For example, when he undertook land ownership in Ireland, and became an Irish landlord, this appeared to be a very profitable venture on his part. But down the line, he did not manage this land properly. And, because of this, he lost most of the fortune that he obtained. This particular mistake was rooted in the mismanagement of his funds.

Like all human being, he would later encounter even more mistakes down the road. For example, when he tried to set up a colony on Roanoke, he made the mistake of not bringing enough supplies and resources with him when he arrived. As a result of this, he was forced to sail back to England, in promise that he would return with everything they needed after one year. However, he became stranded in England, and it took three years instead. He realized he had made a mistake once he returned to Roanoke, and no one was there. However, this did not discourage him.

Another Key mishap involved pursuing an unauthorized marriage, which Queen Elizabeth I did not approve of. As a result of this, both he and she were forced to serve time in a person. However, his biggest mistakes occurred in his later life, and these mistakes seemed to dwarf the failure that occurred at Roanoke.

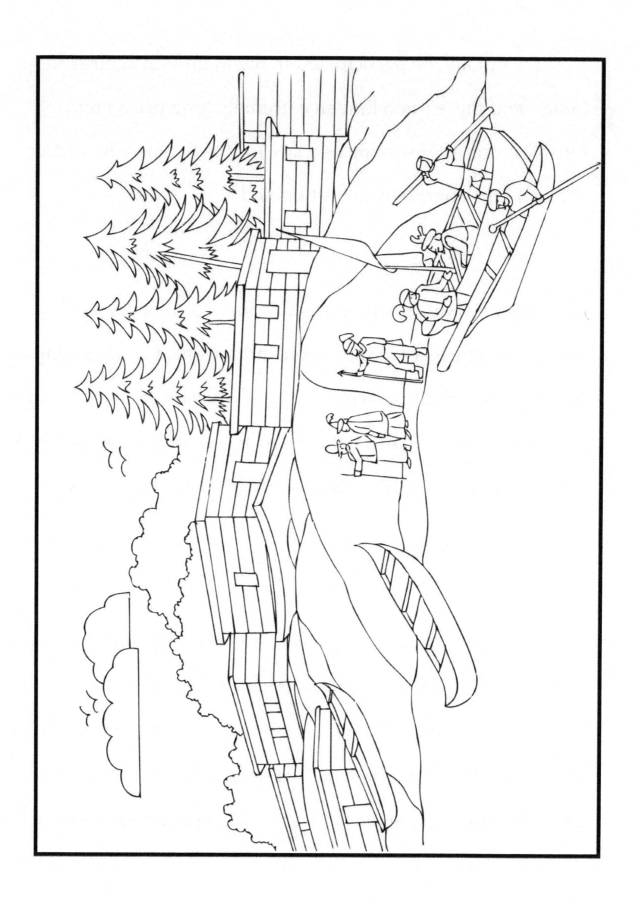

Eventually, he participated in the Main Plot against King James, and this earned him an extremely long prison term. Furthermore, after serving as a spy for the Spanish, he further showed his defiance towards England.

After he was finally released from prison, most would assume that he learned his lesson and refrained from getting into more conflict. But in a twist of fate, he attacked a Spanish fort in Venezuela, and a Spanish ambassador convinced King James to execute him. Eventually, because of his mistakes, he was executed.

Another one of his big mistakes was his unending pursuit of wealth, and greed may have been the cause of some of his greatest misfortunes. There were times during his life when he undertook too many challenges at once, when he pursued to many ambitions all at once. Most of his expeditions were pursued with the expectation that he would find more wealth in the New World.

11. If Walter Raleigh can teach us anything, what is it?

We, as a modern society, truly can learn a lot from Walter Raleigh. One particular lesson that we can learn is that humble beginnings truly do not matter in the scope of what you can accomplish in the future. As stated before, he was born on a farm, and his earliest life was not particularly glamorous in any respect. However, this did not stop him from obtaining an amazing status in society, favor with the Queen, life changing opportunities, and fortune, as well.

Therefore, he is a prime example that with fortitude and persistence, anyone can abandon their humble beginnings, and do really great things in the future.

One of the most impressive things about him is that he obtained his opportunities and took on leadership roles relatively early on in his life. Even though he dropped out of Oriel College after a single year of attendance, this did not deter him from achieving his dreams.

Even in his early days, he participated in the military, rebellions, owned land, and became fairly prominent at a young age. It seems that his desire to exhibit leadership was an inborn trait, but it was most likely fostered by his family upbringing, as well.

As noted, he observed what it meant to voice your beliefs at an early age when his family resisted the Catholic influence. A combination of being a natural born leader and adventurers, and begin exposed to this dynamic, made him one of the most interesting adventurers in history.

While there was no true road to El Dorado, his intrigue and curiosity never made him lose interest in exploration.

12. How did he influence others?

He was known for his ability to lead, charm and persuade others. To consider the influence he may have potentially had on others during the time, it is first important to consider what type of feats he was able to accomplish.

One of his greatest conquests, in the political sense, was that of Queen Elizabeth I. Somehow, he was able to win her favor and her approval over a series of years, and he was appointed to many positions and granted many rewards and opportunities.

Although he incited her wrath once he married one of her ladies in waiting, he had another notable influence on her. He was courteous and charming, and his valor truly won her respect.

From this, it is reasonable to assume that his courage and valor had an awe inspiring effect on those around him. With they see his fearlessness, his courage, and his ability to take a stand, he clearly gained their respect.

How was he able to lead expeditions and thwart his initial plans? Clearly, he was very influential on the men who travelled with him, as well. His ability to lead made other organized, and it made them want to listen to him. Furthermore, the fact that he was able to work secretly with the Spanish shows that he was capable of a great degree of inspiration.

Chapter 9: Timeline

The content in this chapter is intended for use as a historical timeline, which should be used for reference purposes. It compiles all of the most important events that occurred in the life of Sir Walter Raleigh.

- In 1552, Sir Walter Raleigh was born to a Protestant family, in Devonshire, England.

- In 1567 he became a troop member of one hundred horse. He was raised by a family member at the time, and his name was Compte de Montgomerie.

- The year of 1572 was a traumatic day, as he witnessed several French Protestants being killed in large numbers. This is now referred to as the St. Bartholomew Day's Massacre.

- By the year if 1574, he had begun attending Oriel College, which is located in Oxford.

- In 1575, he was inducted into the Middle Temple as a member.

- He and his half brother travelled to America in 1578.

- He has a daughter with a woman named Alice Gold in 1579.

- In 1580, he participated in the Irish rebellion, which he helped end. As a result of this, he gained the favor of Queen Elizabeth and he earned a fortune from the rewards he was given by the Queen.

- In 1581, he started "The School of Night, which was a secret society that he founded.

- By the year 1584, he was given approval to venture into the North American continent and explore. He was also given permission to settle in North America, as well. He reached Roanoke Island with this fleet this very year.

- The year of 1585 was met with more adventure for Sir Walter Raleigh. It was at this time that he became governor of the new territory. He also named the new territory Virginia, to show reverence to the Queen. He was also knighted by the Queen this year.

- In 1586, he realized that someone was trying to assassinate Queen Elizabeth I, and he quickly replaced her.

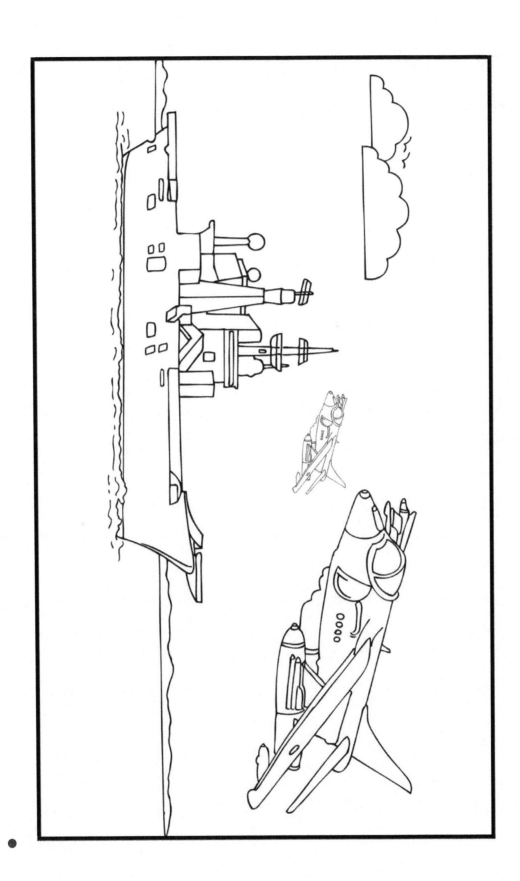

- In 1587, Raleigh was appointed as captain of the Queen's Guard.

- In 1588, Raleigh participated in a rebellion against the Spanish by donating the Ark Royal to the English army.

- In 1592, he marries one of Queen Elizabeth's women in waiting. This makes her very angry and she sends him to prison.

- After he is released, he and his wife have a son named Walter in 1593.

- In 1595, Raleigh leaves England in search of El Dorado in the New World, for it is known to be the city of gold. He never actually finds the city, so, he visits the Orinoco instead.

- In 1600, he becomes the governor or Jersey.

- In 1603, Queen Elizabeth dies and King James rises to power.

- In 1603, King James also sends Raleigh to prison because he wishes to settle things with the Spanish at that time.

- In 1612, he is released from prison to seek out wealth in Guiana, on another expedition.

- In the year of 1616, he never makes it to Guiana. Instead, he attacks a Spanish settlement.
- The Spanish do not take this attack lightly, and he is beheaded in 1618.

```
Z Q K C E W K Y Y N K M C D K
Y Z P N K X O W M K N E R O S
T R D S K U P R A G I G O Y V
E K O N A O R L L N G J U C F
X A Z T H W Y Y O D H H L V W
X Q I J S P F D A R T H E R E
I V R U C I N C L V E E M T U
S V A K B O H K L R D R T A U
E R I E L N R M N Z E L F L K
G Q A P H A E T O W E R X H U
B U B J L Z T O R C D A O N R
D E H E F L L V Y M A H D H R
G Q I U H D A A X M E I A M U
E G V F C X W V V U H K G H A
H W A V A D O I N D L Z O E F
```

CRO
EXPLORER
HISTORY
KNIGHTED
LONDON
RALEIGH
ROANOKE
TOWER
WALTER
WORLD

Get All The Images From This Book

Would you like to color some or all of these images again? Perhaps in different colors or styles. Now you can print out as many copies as you like. I'll send you every design in this book free.

Please just visit
http://coloringfans.com/ raleigh

Thank you so much for purchasing this book. I hope you have many happy hours coloring in all the wonderful images.

Thank you so much again

Made in the USA
Las Vegas, NV
20 December 2020